LIGHTHOUSES

Scott Benjamin Gracie

In Lumine Stellas

A catalogue record for this
book is available from the
National Library of Australia

NATIONAL
LIBRARY
OF AUSTRALIA

ISBN
978-0-6456241-2-0 (Hardcover)
978-0-6456241-3-7 (eBook)

LIGHTHOUSES

This collection of images presents many different types of lighthouses from around the world.

Some are beautiful, or in amazing locations, and some extraordinarily remote. Some are painted different colours, while others are bare and showing their natural materials. But all have one singular purpose of protecting seafarers from danger by guiding them along a safe path, using the wonder of light.

This book offers a captivating journey through the world of lighthouses. Towering sentinels of our waterways and oceans that have guided sailors through treacherous conditions for centuries.

From the rugged cliffs of Scotland to the serene shores of the Mediterranean, these guardians of the sea, stand as symbols of safety, hope, and the enduring battle against nature's might.

Scott Benjamin Gracie

Table of Contents

Introduction

The history of lighthouses is a fascinating journey through time, technology, and maritime navigation. It spans over two millennia and reflects the changing needs and capabilities of seafaring cultures across the world.

Ancient Beginnings - The earliest known lighthouses were simple bonfires built on hillsides to guide ships to port. However, the most iconic early lighthouse was the Pharos of Alexandria, Egypt, built in the third century BCE. This remarkable structure stood over 100 meters tall and was considered one of the Seven Wonders of the Ancient World. It used an open flame at its top, magnified by mirrors during the day and burning brightly at night.

Roman Contributions - The Romans inherited the concept of lighthouses from the Greeks and expanded on it. They built lighthouses across their empire, including notable ones at Dover, England, and La Coruña, Spain. These structures were often more utilitarian than the Pharos, built for function over form, but they were crucial in ensuring the safety of the extensive Roman maritime trade.

Medieval Developments - During the Middle Ages, the construction of lighthouses slowed significantly. However, existing lighthouses were maintained and some new ones were built, particularly in important maritime nations like Italy and Spain. These lighthouses were often run by local authorities or religious orders, and the technology remained relatively static, relying primarily on open fires or candles.

The Age of Exploration - The Age of Exploration in the 15th and 16th centuries led to a resurgence in lighthouse construction. As European powers competed for naval dominance and new trade routes, the importance of effective maritime navigation became paramount. Notable lighthouses of this era include those at Cape St. Vincent, Portugal, and on the island of Madeira.

Technological Advances in the 18th and 19th Centuries - The 18th and 19th centuries saw significant technological advancements in lighthouse construction and lighting methods. The invention of the Fresnel lens in the early 19th century was a major breakthrough, allowing for the creation of brighter and more focused beams of light. Lighthouses became taller, more durable, and more efficient, with many iconic structures like the Eddystone Lighthouse in England and the Statue of Liberty in the USA (originally serving as a lighthouse) being constructed during this period.

20th Century and Beyond - The 20th century brought electrification, automated lamps, and eventually solar power, making lighthouses more reliable and easier to maintain. During this time, lighthouses began to lose some of their traditional importance due to advances in navigation technology, such as GPS. However, they remain critical in many areas for safe maritime travel and have also become cultural and historical landmarks.

The history of lighthouses mirrors the history of maritime exploration, trade, and technology. From ancient wonders to modern automated beacons, lighthouses have not only ensured the safety of mariners but have also become enduring symbols of guidance and resilience against the forces of nature. Their story is a testament to human ingenuity and the relentless pursuit of safe passage through the vast and unpredictable oceans and waterways.

Montaza Palace Lighthouse
Alexandria, Egypt

Peggys Cove Lighthouse
Nova Scotia, Canada

Les Eclaireurs Lighthouse
Eclaireurs, Ushuaia, Tierra del Fuego, Argentina

Beachy Head Lighthouse
Eastbourne, England, United Kingdom

Point of Ayr Lighthouse
Talacre Beach, Talacre, Wales, United Kingdom

Tower of Hercules Lighthouse
A Coruña Harbour, Galicia, Spain

Vyborg Bay Lighthouse
Vyborgskiy Zaliv, Leningrad Region, Russia

The Lighthouse of Rethymnon
Rethymno Harbour, Rethymno, Crete, Greece

La Madonetta Lighthouse
Harbour of Bonifacio, Corsica, France

Landsort Lighthouse
Öja island, Landsort, Stockholm, Sweden

North Head Lighthouse
Ilwaco, Washington, United States

Mannar Lighthouse
Mannar, northern coast of Sri Lanka

Aniva lighthouse
Sakhalin Region, Russia

Nieuwe Sluis, Breskens Lighthouse
Breskens, Netherland

Tillamook Head Lighthouse
Tillamook Head, Ecola State Park, Oregon, United States

Macquarie Lighthouse
Vaucluse, Sydney, New South Wales, Australia

Plymouth Breakwater Lighthouse
Plymouth, England, United Kingdom

Lighthouses stand as timeless sentinels, guardians of the treacherous and the tranquil, guiding mariners through the ages with their unwavering lights. These iconic structures, perched on rugged cliffs, nestled on sandy shores, or standing solitary on distant isles, weave a rich tapestry of history, technology, and human endeavour. The story of lighthouses is as much about the people who built and maintained them as it is about the advancements in engineering and navigation they represent. This book aims to explore the multifaceted narrative of lighthouses, illuminating their evolution from ancient fire on wooden platforms to sophisticated, automated beacons that continue to guide ships in the 21st century.

In the ancient world, the first lighthouses emerged not just as navigational aids but as symbols of power and technological prowess. The Pharos of Alexandria, one of the Seven Wonders of the Ancient World, epitomizes the importance of these early beacons, serving both as a guiding light and a monumental testament to Hellenistic engineering. When looking a lighthouses through the centuries, we witness the transformation of lighthouses from simple bonfires to architectural marvels equipped with cutting-edge technology.

The Middle Ages saw the proliferation of lighthouses across Europe, albeit in a more modest form compared to the grandeur of ancient times. These were dark times for maritime navigation, yet the flickering lights of lighthouses offered a glimmer of hope, a promise of safe harbor. It was during the Renaissance and the Age of Discovery that lighthouses regained their prominence. The explosion of maritime trade and exploration underscored the need for reliable navigational aids, leading to significant advancements in lighthouse construction and lighting technology.

The Industrial Revolution brought about a new era of innovation in lighthouse technology. The invention of the Fresnel lens, a masterpiece of optical engineering, revolutionized lighthouse illumination, projecting beams of light far into the horizon. This period also saw the construction of some of the most iconic lighthouses, engineering feats that defied the elements and stood as symbols of human perseverance and ingenuity.

In the modern era, the story of lighthouses transcends their functional role as navigational aids. It is a story of automation and obsolescence, of preservation and adaptation. As electronic navigation systems like GPS became prevalent, the traditional role of lighthouses diminished. Yet, their cultural and historical significance only grew, with many being preserved as monuments to maritime heritage, attracting visitors from around the world.

This book is an ode to lighthouses, those enduring beacons of light that have captivated the human imagination for centuries. It is a story of innovation, resilience, and the unbreakable bond between humanity and the sea. While some lighthouses in this book were built centuries ago, and others being more modern, all have unique characteristics and charm. Lighthouses, with their rich history and enduring presence, remind us of the power of light to guide, to warn, and to inspire.

St. Mary's Lighthouse
Whitley Bay, Hartley, England, United Kingdom

Kiel Holtenau Lighthouse
Kiel, Schleswig-Holstein, Germany

Southern Breakwater Lighthouse
Southern Breakwater, Port of Dover, Kent, England, United Kingdom

Westerheversand Lighthouse
Westerheversand, Schleswig-Holstein, Germany

Chipiona Lighthouse
Chipiona, Cádiz, Spain

Chania Lighthouse
Chania, Crete, Greece

Coquet Island Lighthouse
Amble, Northumberland, England, United Kingdom

Kjeungskjær Lighthouse/ The Red Sailor
Uthaug, Trøndelag, Norway

Point Cabrillo Lighthouse
Mendocino, California, United States

Chicago Harbour Lighthouse
Chicago, Illinois, United States

Rubha Reidh Lighthouse
Melvaig, Gairloch, Wester Ross, Scotland, United Kingdom

Big Tub Lighthouse
Tobermory, Bruce Peninsula, Ontario, Canada

Sambro Island Lighthouse
Sambro Island, Halifax, Nova Scotia, Canada

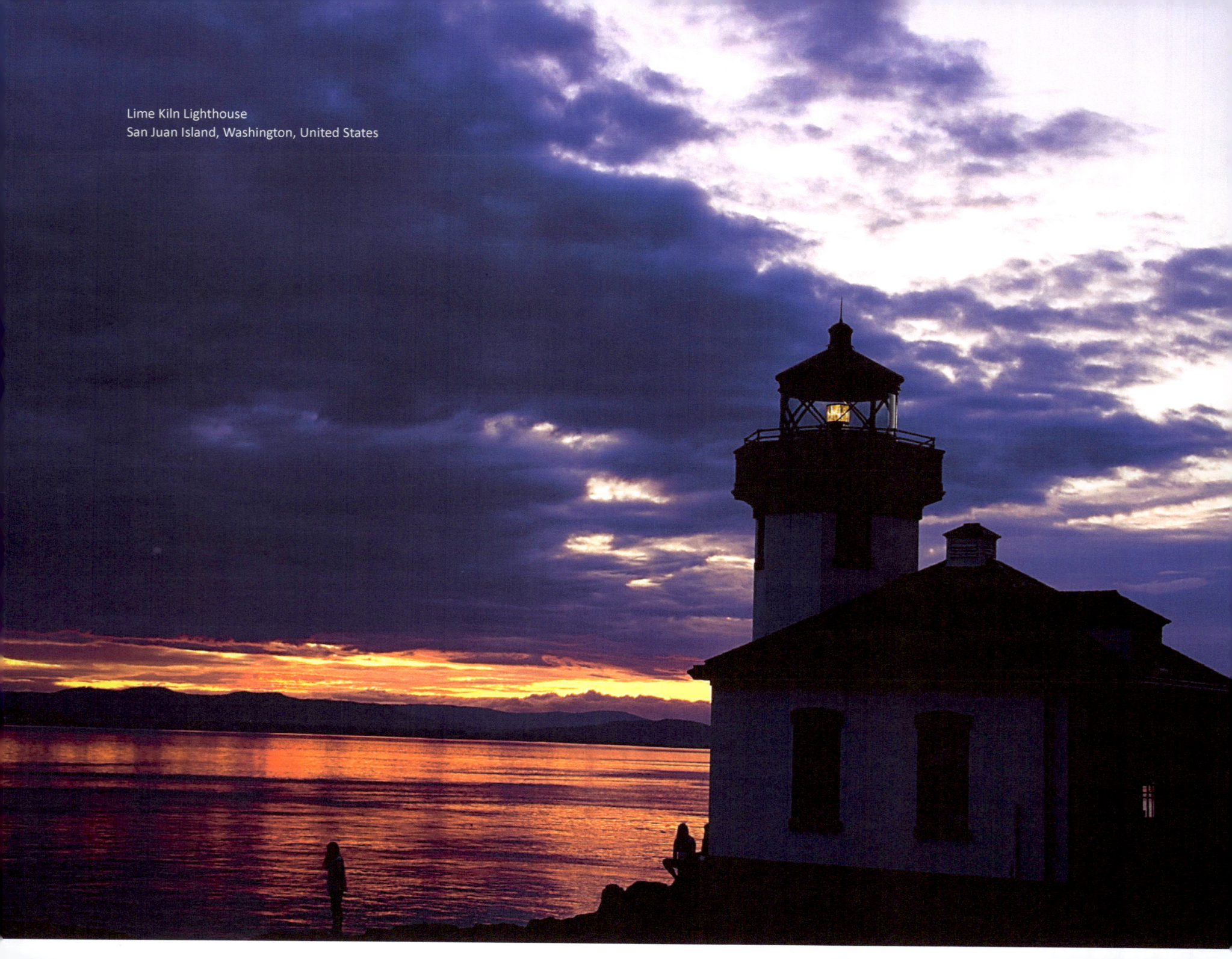

Lime Kiln Lighthouse
San Juan Island, Washington, United States

Bressay Llighthouse
Bressay, Kirkabister Ness, Scotland, United Kingdom

Saint George Reef Lighthouse
Crescent City, California, United States

St Anthony's Lighthouse
St Anthony's Beach, Truro, England, United Kingdom

Little Ross Lighthouse
Little Ross Island, Kirkcudbright, Scotland, United Kingdom

Les Eclaireurs Lighthouse
Canal Beagle, Ushuaia, Tierra del Fuego, Argentina

Capo Testa lighthouse
Capo Testa, Sardinia, Italy

Ponta dos Capelinhos Lighthouse
Faial Island, Capelo, Azores

Skerries Lighthouse
The Skerries, Isle of Anglesey, England, United Kingdom

Lighthouse architecture, with its rich diversity and ingenuity, spans a wide spectrum of designs, each tailored to its specific environment and technological era. These structures, often situated in some of the most challenging and picturesque locations on the planet, are not just functional navigational aids but also architectural marvels that reflect the cultural, historical, and technological contexts of their times. The design of a lighthouse is influenced by various factors, including the need for visibility from sea and land, durability against harsh weather conditions, and the accommodation of keepers and equipment.

The foundational aspect of lighthouse architecture is its structure and form. Traditionally, lighthouses are tall, tower-like buildings designed to elevate the light source, ensuring its visibility over long distances and above obstructions like cliffs or buildings. The shape of the tower is often conical or cylindrical, which offers resistance to strong winds and waves, especially in coastal or offshore locations. Materials used in construction have evolved from wood and stone in early lighthouses to brick, concrete, and steel in modern ones, chosen for their durability and resistance to the elements.

One of the most iconic architectural elements of a lighthouse is the lantern room, which houses the light source and optics. This glass-enclosed space is usually situated at the top of the tower, designed to maximize the light's visibility in all directions. The lantern room often features a distinctive shape and design, such as a decagonal or circular form, and is sometimes capped with a domed or conical roof. Surrounding the lantern room, outdoor galleries or walkways allow for maintenance access and provide stunning views for the lighthouse keepers.

Below the lantern room, the tower's interior is designed with functionality in mind. Spiral staircases or, in some modern lighthouses, elevators allow for access to the top. The interior space also accommodates the workings of the light mechanism, such as the rotation gear and power supply, and, in older lighthouses, living quarters for the keepers. These living spaces were essential in remote locations, providing keepers and their families with accommodations, often for extended periods.

The base of the lighthouse, or the keeper's house in some designs, is integrated into the tower or constructed separately. These structures were built to provide additional living, working, and storage space. In design, they often reflect the architectural styles of their periods and regions, ranging from simple, functional forms to elaborate styles with decorative elements.

Architecturally, lighthouses are also designed to symbolize their importance and the cultural value placed on maritime safety. Some feature elaborate ornamentation, such as stonework, masonry details, or even sculptures, that reflect local traditions and craftsmanship. The colour and pattern of a lighthouse—its daymark—are not arbitrary but carefully chosen to stand out against the background landscape and seascape, further enhancing its visibility and functionality as a navigational aid.

Lighthouse architecture, in essence, represents a harmonious blend of form and function, designed to withstand the test of time and nature. These structures not only serve as vital aids to navigation but also as cultural and historical landmarks, celebrated for their beauty, resilience, and the stories they hold within their walls.

Chanonry Point Lighthouse
Chanonry Point, Rosemarkie Bay, Scotland, United Kingdom

Whitby Harbour East Lighthouse
Whitby, England, United Kingdom

Muckle Flugga Lighthouse
Muckle Flugga, Shetland, Scotland, United Kingdom

Murano Lighthouse
Venezia, Venice, Italy

Bugio Tower Lighthouse
River Tagus, Oeiras, Portugal

Cape Saint Vincent Lighthouse
Sagres Point, Sagres, Vila do Bispo, Portugal

Rubh An Duin Lighthouse
Port Charlotte, Isle of Islay, Scotland, United Kingdom

Maidens East Tower Lighthouse
Larne, North Channel, Northern Ireland United Kingdom

Neist Point Lighthouse
Neist Point, Skye, Scotland, United Kingdom

Punta Cavazzi Lighthouse
Ustica, Metropolitan City of Palermo, Italy

Almadies Lighthouse
Les Almadies, Dakar, Senegal, Africa

Tynemouth Pier Lighthouse
Tynemouth, North Shields, England, United Kingdom

Los Angeles Harbor Lighthouse
San Pedro, California, United States

Tiumpan Head Lighthouse
Stornoway, Isle of Lewis, Scotland, United Kingdom

Oksøy Lighthouse
Oksøy, Flekkerøy, Norway

Cap Formentor Lighthouse
Pollença, Mallorca, Balearic Islands, Spain

Hopsnes Lighthouse
Grindavik, Suðurnes, Iceland

St Abbs Lighthouse
Coldingham, Eyemouth, Scotland, United Kingdom

Morro Lighthouse
Porto Cristo, Manacor, Mallorca, Spain

Fanad Head Lighthouse
Fanad Head, Donegal County, Ireland

Eilean Musdile Lighthouse,
Eilean Musdile, Lismore, Scotland, United Kingdom

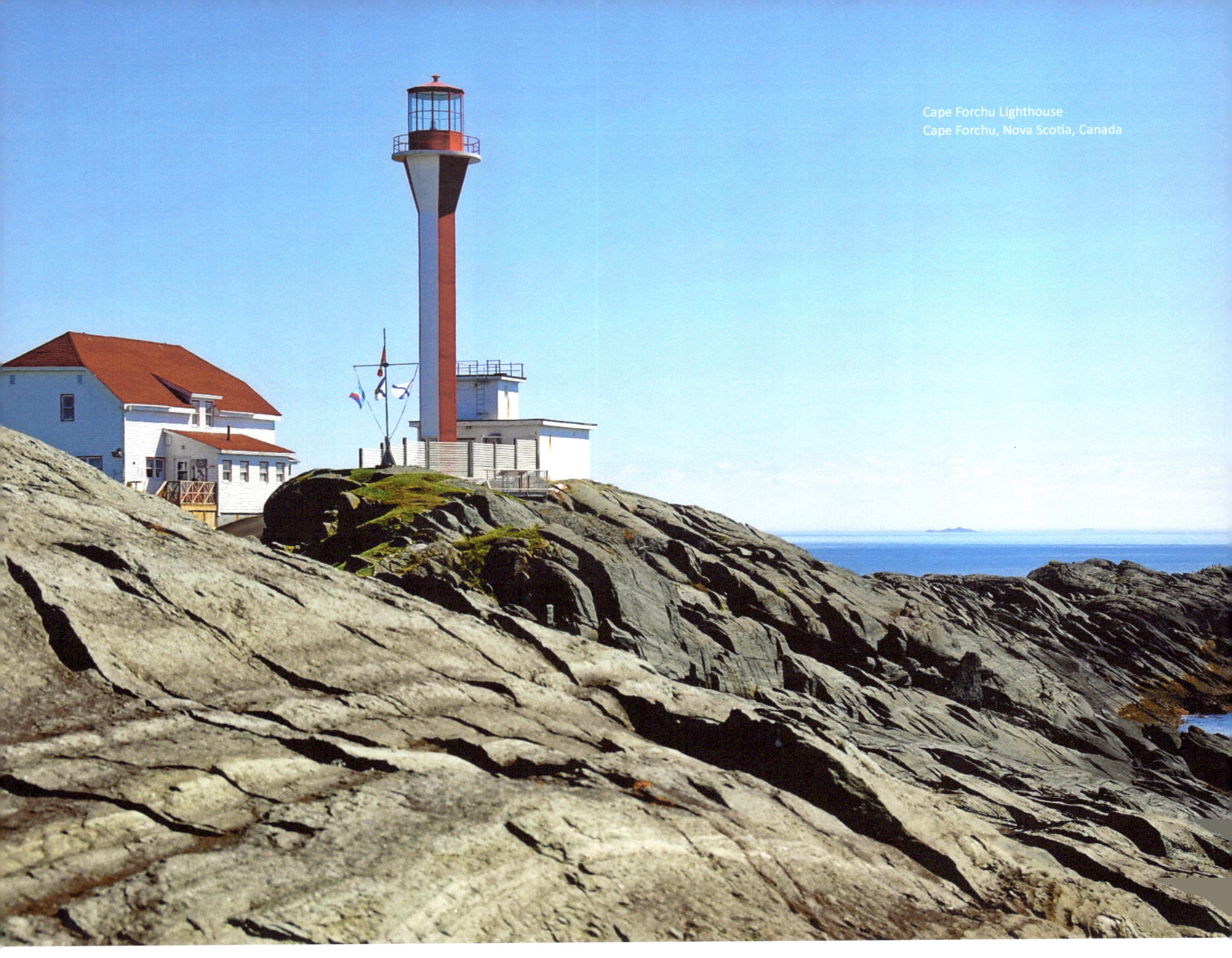

Cape Forchu Lighthouse
Cape Forchu, Nova Scotia, Canada

Black Rock Point Lighthouse
Black Rock, Nova Scotia, Canada

Tobermory Lighthouse
Tobermory, Isle of Mull, Scotland, United Kingdom

Lighthouses have employed a fascinating array of mechanisms and technologies to fulfill their critical role. From ancient fires to modern automated systems, the evolution of lighthouses reflects centuries of innovation in optics, engineering, and energy sources.

At the heart of a lighthouse's functionality is its light source, which has evolved significantly over time. Ancient lighthouses used open fires or torches, often fuelled by wood, coal, or oil, to produce light. These early sources were effective but limited in range and reliability. The introduction of candles and later oil lamps in the Middle Ages offered improvements, but the true transformation in lighthouse illumination came with the advent of more sophisticated fuels and technologies, including kerosene and, eventually, electric lights. Electric lighting, introduced in the late 19th and early 20th centuries, marked a significant leap forward, offering brighter, more reliable light sources that could be seen from greater distances.

The optical system of a lighthouse, designed to focus and intensify the light, is another central part of how a lighthouse operates. The invention of the Fresnel lens in the 1820s by French physicist Augustin-Jean Fresnel was a revolutionary advancement. The Fresnel lens consists of multiple annular sections of glass, arranged in a beehive shape, which capture and redirect light toward the horizon. This design significantly increased the intensity and reach of the lighthouse beam, enabling it to guide ships from much farther away. Different orders of Fresnel lenses were developed, varying in size and light range, to suit different needs and locations.

Rotating mechanisms are employed in many lighthouses to create a distinctive flash pattern or characteristic, allowing mariners to identify their location along the coast or in relation to other navigational landmarks. Originally, these mechanisms involved clockwork-driven or weight-powered systems, where the keeper would wind up a mechanism that would slowly rotate the lens or light source. In modern lighthouses, electric motors now perform this function, but the principle remains the same: creating identifiable sequences of flashes or beams that can be recognized and relied upon.

Sound-emitting mechanisms, such as foghorns, complement the visual guidance provided by lighthouses. These are especially crucial in foggy or stormy conditions when visibility is poor. Early fog signals ranged from cannons to bells, while modern versions use compressed air or electronic systems to generate powerful, penetrating sounds.

Lighthouse power sources have also evolved, from manual efforts to advanced technologies. Early lighthouses relied on the physical labour of keepers for everything from lighting the lamps to operating the rotation mechanism. With the advent of electricity, lighthouses became more autonomous, a trend that culminated in the automation of the 20th century. Today, many lighthouses are powered by solar panels, battery banks, or even wind turbines, making them more environmentally friendly and reducing the need for constant human intervention.

The mechanisms of lighthouses, from their light sources and optical systems to their power supplies and sound signals, represent a blend of historical innovation and modern technology. These systems have been refined over centuries to ensure that lighthouses remain reliable aids to navigation, continuing their mission to safeguard the maritime journey of vessels around the globe.

Cape Otway Lighthouse
Cape Otway, Victoria, Australia

Girdle Ness Lighthouse
Balnagask, Aberdeen, Scotland, United Kingdom

The Mull of Galloway Lighthouse
Cairngaan, Scotland, United Kingdom

Pointe-à-la-Renommée Lighthouse
Ruisseau-à-l'Ail, Gaspé, Quebec, Canada

Okunoshima Lighthouse
Tadanoumicho, Okunoshima Island, Japan

Høgsteinen Lighthouse
Giske Municipality, Godøya, Norway

Each lighthouse has its own history and tales to tell. Among these, several have gained fame not only for their architectural beauty and historical significance but also for their roles in maritime safety and cultural lore.

Pharos of Alexandria, Egypt - Once considered one of the Seven Wonders of the Ancient World, the Pharos of Alexandria was constructed in the 3rd century BC on the island of Pharos. Though it no longer stands, its legacy as one of the earliest and tallest lighthouses in history, reaching heights possibly between 100 and 140 meters, has left an indelible mark on maritime history. It served as a model and inspiration for lighthouse builders throughout the ages.

Eddystone Lighthouse, England - Situated on the perilous Eddystone Rocks, 14 km off the coast of Devon, England, the current structure is the fourth to be built on the site since 1698. The lighthouse is famed for its engineering feats against the odds of nature. John Smeaton's tower, the third built and the first to use interlocking stone blocks, marked a significant advance in lighthouse design when it was erected in 1759.

Bell Rock Lighthouse, Scotland - Off the coast of Angus, Scotland, stands the world's oldest surviving sea-washed lighthouse, completed in 1811 by Robert Stevenson. Built on the treacherous Bell Rock reef, which is submerged at high tide, its construction is a tale of engineering brilliance and human endurance. The lighthouse's design and construction techniques were pioneering at the time and have influenced lighthouse construction ever since.

Cape Hatteras Lighthouse, USA - Known for its distinctive black and white spiral pattern, the Cape Hatteras Lighthouse in North Carolina is the tallest brick lighthouse in the United States, standing at 64 meters. It was built in 1870 to warn ships of the dangerous Diamond Shoals, a notorious area off the Atlantic coast. In an impressive feat of engineering, the lighthouse was moved 870 meters inland in 1999 to protect it from the encroaching sea.

Peggy's Point Lighthouse, Canada - Located in the picturesque village of Peggy's Cove, Nova Scotia, this lighthouse is one of Canada's most well-known and photographed landmarks. Built in 1915, its iconic white and red structure stands on a granite outcrop, overlooking the Atlantic. While it is still operational, the lighthouse has also become a symbol of the rugged beauty and maritime heritage of Nova Scotia.

Montauk Point Lighthouse, USA - As New York's oldest lighthouse and the fourth oldest active lighthouse in the United States, Montauk Point Lighthouse has been guiding ships since 1796. Commissioned by President George Washington, it stands at the easternmost point of Long Island, New York. The lighthouse has become an emblem of Long Island's maritime history and is a popular historical site.

Kõpu Lighthouse, Estonia - One of the oldest lighthouses in the world, Kõpu Lighthouse, has been in continuous operation since its completion in 1531 on the island of Hiiumaa. It was built to assist ships navigating the Baltic Sea and is notable for its historical significance and resilience, having served mariners for nearly five centuries.

Akrotiri Lighthouse
Santorini, Greece

New Lindau Lighthouse
Hafen, Lindau, Germany

South Stack Lighthouse
South Stack, Wales, United Kingdom

Ploumanac'h Lighthouse
Ploumanac'h, Perros-Guirec, France

Statue of Liberty Lighthouse
New York City, New York, United States

Beacon on the seafront
Withernsea, England, United Kingdom

Acknowledgements

Thank you to the all the photographers who helped make this book possible. Their wonderful images, quite often taken for cataloguing purposes, are some of the most unique and inspiring works of photography,

Image Credits

P.2 Mohamed Attia Abd El Aziz
https://commons.wikimedia.org/wiki/File:DSC_4XDX381.jpg

P.3 Shawn M. Kent
https://commons.wikimedia.org/wiki/File:Peggys_Cove_Lighthouse,_NS.jpg

P.4 UCaetano
https://commons.wikimedia.org/wiki/File:Patagonia-leseclarieus.jpg

P.5 Ian Capper
https://commons.wikimedia.org/wiki/File:Beachy_Head_Lighthouse_-_geograph.org.uk_-_4942067.jpg

P.6 Jeff Buck
https://commons.wikimedia.org/wiki/File:Point_of_Ayr_Lighthouse_-_geograph.org.uk_-_3351570.jpg

P.7 Senza Senso
https://commons.wikimedia.org/wiki/File:Lighthouse_Torre_de_H%C3%A9rcules_(Tower_of_Hercules)_(21661683502).jpg

P.8 Владимир Максимов
https://commons.wikimedia.org/wiki/File:%D0%A0%D0%B5%D0%B2%D1%83%D0%BD_-_panoramio.jpg

P.9 Jebulon
https://commons.wikimedia.org/wiki/File:Harbour_snowy_mountains_Rethymno_Crete_Greece.jpg

P.10 Myrabella
https://commons.wikimedia.org/wiki/File:Bonifacio_phare_Madonetta_2.jpg

P.11 ArildV
https://commons.wikimedia.org/wiki/File:Landsort_lighthouse_2012b.jpg

P.12 Mattsjc
https://commons.wikimedia.org/wiki/File:North_Head_Lighthouse_at_Cape_Disappointment.jpg

P.13 Chinthana Prabhashitha Rajapaksha
https://commons.wikimedia.org/wiki/File:Mannar_Lighthouse.jpg

P.14. Ashley Dace
https://commons.wikimedia.org/wiki/File:Happisburgh_Lighthouse_-_geograph.org.uk_-_2078723.jpg

P.15 Yaroslav Shuraev
https://commons.wikimedia.org/wiki/File:%D0%9C%D0%B0%D1%8F%D0%BA_%D0%90%D0%BD%D0%B8%D0%B2%D0%B0.jpg

P.16 Michielverbeek
https://commons.wikimedia.org/wiki/File:Nieuwe_Sluis,_vuurtoren_RM31526_foto6_2015-09-25_12.49.jpg

P.17 Oregon State Archives
https://commons.wikimedia.org/wiki/File:Ecola_State_Park,_Tillamook_Head_Lighthouse,_Tillamook_Head_-_DPLA_-_7102352e25f0b74a14101e115da3774e.jpg

P.18 Sardaka
https://commons.wikimedia.org/wiki/File:1_Macquarie_Lighthouse1.JPG

P.19 Peter S
https://commons.wikimedia.org/wiki/File:Lighthouse_on_Plymouth_Breakwater_-_geograph.org.uk_-_4626876.jpg

P.20 Walter Baxter
https://commons.wikimedia.org/wiki/File:The_Isle_of_May_Lighthouse_-_geograph.org.uk_-_2964179.jpg

P.21 Fraser Darrah
https://commons.wikimedia.org/wiki/File:St._Mary%27s_Lighthouse_from_Hartley_-_geograph.org.uk_-_2081815.jpg

P.22 Ichwarsnur
https://commons.wikimedia.org/wiki/File:Kiel_Holtenau_Leuchtturm_Luftbildaufnahme_Schleuse.jpg

P.23 Tim Glover
https://commons.wikimedia.org/wiki/File:Lighthouse,_Southern_Breakwater_-_geograph.org.uk_-_5866007.jpg

P.24 H. Zell
https://commons.wikimedia.org/wiki/File:Westerhever.jpg

P.25 Diego Delso
https://commons.wikimedia.org/wiki/File:Faro,_Chipiona,_Espa%C3%B1a,_2015-12-08,_DD_24.JPG

P.26 Marc Ryckaert
https://commons.wikimedia.org/wiki/File:Chania_Lighthouse_R01.jpg

P.27 Andrew Curtis
https://commons.wikimedia.org/wiki/File:Lighthouse,_Coquet_Island_-_geograph.org.uk_-_2918917.jpg

P.28 Gordon Leggett
https://commons.wikimedia.org/wiki/File:2016-11-13_02_Kjeungskj%C3%A6r_Lighthouse,_S%C3%B8r-Tr%C3%B8ndelag,_Norway.jpg

P.29 Frank Schulenburg
https://commons.wikimedia.org/wiki/File:Point_Cabrillo_Lighthouse,_on_an_early_morning_in_February.jpg

P.30 Alex Ford
https://commons.wikimedia.org/wiki/File:Lighthouse_on_Lake_Michigan_(3519226935).jpg

P.31 Bill Kasman
https://commons.wikimedia.org/wiki/File:Rubha_Reidh_lighthouse_-_geograph.org.uk_-_5286838.jpg

P.32 Chen Feng
https://commons.wikimedia.org/wiki/File:Tobermory_Lighthouse_-_panoramio_(2).jpg

P.33 Dennis Jarvis
https://commons.wikimedia.org/wiki/File:Sambro_Island_Lighthouse_%284%29.jpg

P.34 NormsDiner
https://commons.wikimedia.org/wiki/File:Lime_Kiln_Lighthouse_at_Sunset.jpg

P.35 Borowski eric
https://commons.wikimedia.org/wiki/File:P_Pan_HDR_REV_Bass_Rock_01_IMG_0941_6i.jpg

P.36 Chris Downer
https://commons.wikimedia.org/wiki/File:Bressay,_Kirkabister_Ness_lighthouse_-_geograph.org.uk_-_2655917.jpg

P.37 Raquel Baranow
https://commons.wikimedia.org/wiki/File:Saint_
George_Reef_Lighthouse_3.jpg

P.38 August Schwerdfeger
https://commons.wikimedia.org/wiki/File:St._Ant
hony%27s_Lighthouse_as_viewed_from_Penden
nis_Point_2019-06-04.jpg

P.39 Neil Theasby
https://commons.wikimedia.org/wiki/File:Little_R
oss_Lighthouse_-_geograph.org.uk_-
_5502437.jpg

P.40 UCaetano
https://commons.wikimedia.org/wiki/File:Patago
nia-leseclarieus.jpg

P.41 Diana Robinson
https://www.flickr.com/photos/dianasch/451529
49435/in/photostream/

P.42 Unukorno
https://commons.wikimedia.org/wiki/File:Faial_F
arol_da_Ponta_dos_Capelinhos_01.jpg

P.43 Stephen Elwyn Roddick
https://commons.wikimedia.org/wiki/File:Skerrie
s_Lighthouse_from_Ynys_Arw_-
geograph.org.uk-_4563012.jpg

P.44 Farajiibrahim
https://commons.wikimedia.org/wiki/File:Lightho
use_of_RAS_OUREK_-_Cap_des_trois_fourches_-
_Nador_Morocco_-_Brahim_FARAJI.jpg

P.45 Greg Fitchett
https://commons.wikimedia.org/wiki/File:Sunrise
_at_Chanonry_Point_lighthouse_-
geograph.org.uk-_4207150.jpg

P.46 Rick Harrison
https://www.flickr.com/photos/sovietuk/3164995
242

P.47 Pjt56
https://commons.wikimedia.org/wiki/File:Muckle
FluggaLighthouse-pjt.jpg

P.48 GodeNehler
https://commons.wikimedia.org/wiki/File:Venedi
g_ACTV_Stop_Murano_Faro-4235.jpg

P.49 Pedro S Bello
https://commons.wikimedia.org/wiki/File:Oeiras_
-_Bugio_03.jpg

P.50 Matthias Süßen
https://commons.wikimedia.org/wiki/File:Silves-
Ponte-2019-msu-2351.jpg

P.51 M J Richardson
https://commons.wikimedia.org/wiki/File:Rubh%
27an_D%C3%B9in_lighthouse_-
geograph.org.uk-_4003510.jpg

P.52 Diego Delso
https://commons.wikimedia.org/wiki/File:Faro_d
el_cabo_Espartel,_Marruecos,_2015-12-
11,_DD_02.JPG

P.53 David Dixon
https://commons.wikimedia.org/wiki/File:The_M
aidens_Lighthouse_-_geograph.org.uk_-
_5761798.jpg

P.54 Bob Embleton
https://commons.wikimedia.org/wiki/File:Neist_P
oint_Lighthouse_-_geograph.org.uk_-
_2015045.jpg

P.55 Chris Heaton
https://commons.wikimedia.org/wiki/File:Coastal
_View_from_Black_Point_-_geograph.org.uk_-
_3920774.jpg

P.56 Stephen kleckner
https://commons.wikimedia.org/wiki/File:Faro_di
_punta_Gavassi_visto_dall%27Isola_di_Ustica_by
_Stephen_Kleckner.jpg

P.57 Charlottedkr
https://commons.wikimedia.org/wiki/File:Phare_
des_Almadies.jpg

P.58 Colin Smith
https://commons.wikimedia.org/wiki/File:Tynem
outh_Pier_Lighthouse_-_geograph.org.uk_-
_3136407.jpg

P.59 Lam094
https://commons.wikimedia.org/wiki/File:Los_An
geles_Harbor_Lighthouse.jpg

P.60 Peter Moore
https://commons.wikimedia.org/wiki/File:Tiumpa
n_Head_Lighthouse_-_geograph.org.uk_-
_4662740.jpg

P.61 Petter Ulleland
https://commons.wikimedia.org/wiki/File:Oks%C
3%B8y_fyr_juni_2018_(4).jpg

P.62 Taxiarchos228
https://commons.wikimedia.org/wiki/File:Mallorc
a_-_Leuchtturm_am_Kap_Formentor2.jpg

P.63 Diego Delso
https://commons.wikimedia.org/wiki/File:Faro_d
e_Hopsnes,_Su%C3%B0urland,_Islandia,_2014-
08-13,_DD_082.JPG

P.64 Graham Robson
https://commons.wikimedia.org/wiki/File:Lookin
g_down_on_St_Abbs_Lighthouse_-
geograph.org.uk-_4531625.jpg

P.65 A.Savin
https://commons.wikimedia.org/wiki/File:Mallorc
a_Porto_Cristo_seaport_area_asv2023-
04_img5.jpg

P.66 Suicasmo
https://commons.wikimedia.org/wiki/File:Kaohsi
ung_Lighthouse_20141010.jpg

P.67 Rossographer
https://commons.wikimedia.org/wiki/File:Fanad_
Head_Lighthouse_-_geograph.org.uk_-
_5731201.jpg

P.68 Ian S
https://commons.wikimedia.org/wiki/File:Eilean_
Musdile_Lighthouse,_Lismore_-
geograph.org.uk-_5210927.jpg

P.69 Dennis Jarvis
https://www.flickr.com/photos/archer10/609978
0377

P.70 Dennis Jarvis
https://www.flickr.com/photos/archer10/635352
3657

P.71 Chen Feng
https://commons.wikimedia.org/wiki/File:Toberm
ory_Lighthouse_-_panoramio_(2).jpg

P.72 Thomas Nugent
https://commons.wikimedia.org/wiki/File:Perch_l
ighthouse_-_geograph.org.uk_-_337674.jpg

P.73 Marc Ryckaert
https://commons.wikimedia.org/wiki/File:Corfu_
Lighthouse_R01.jpg

P.74 Dietmar Rabich
https://commons.wikimedia.org/wiki/File:Cape_
Otway_%28AU%29,_Cape_Otway_Lighthouse_--
_2019_--_1239.jpg

P.75 Greig Ritchie
https://commons.wikimedia.org/wiki/File:Girdlen
ess_Lighthouse_Aberdeen_-_geograph.org.uk_-
_1958001.jpg

P.76 Chris McAuley
https://commons.wikimedia.org/wiki/File:The_M
ull_of_Galloway_Lighthouse_-_geograph.org.uk_-
_3194452.jpg

P.77 Dennis Jarvis
https://www.flickr.com/photos/archer10/497128
7829/in/album-72157603858415319/

P.78 Steffen Flor
https://commons.wikimedia.org/wiki/File:Lightho
use_in_Okunoshima,_August_2018.jpg

P.79 Gordon Leggett
https://commons.wikimedia.org/wiki/File:2023-
0518_01_H%C3%B8gsteinen_Lighthouse_(H%C3
%B8gsteinen_fyrstasjon,_view_from_north),_Nor
way.jpg

P.80 David Dixon
https://commons.wikimedia.org/wiki/File:Fidra_L
ighthouse_-_geograph.org.uk_-_5422478.jpg

P.81 Moonik
https://commons.wikimedia.org/wiki/File:Santori
ni_lighthouse,_Greece_001.jpg

P.82 Kritzolina
https://commons.wikimedia.org/wiki/File:Die_Sc
hwaben_bei_der_Einfahrt_in_den_Lindauer_Haf
en_02.jpg

P.83 Oliver Mills
https://commons.wikimedia.org/wiki/File:South_
Stack_Lighthouse_-_geograph.org.uk_-
_4585123.jpg

P.84 Rui Glória
https://commons.wikimedia.org/wiki/File:Cabo_d
e_S%C3%A3o_Vicente_-_Sagres.jpg

P.85 Philippe Serrand
https://www.pexels.com/photo/a-lighthouse-sits-
on-top-of-a-rocky-outcrop-18382373/

P.86 Dietmar Rabich
https://commons.wikimedia.org/wiki/File:New_Y
ork_City_(New_York,_USA),_Statue_of_Liberty_--
_2012_--_6814.jpg

P.87 Malc McDonald
https://www.geograph.org.uk/photo/6879970